Tikal: The History of the Ancient Maya's Famous Capital

By Jesse Harasta and Charles River Editors

One of the temples at Tikal. Photo by Raymond Ostertag.

About Charles River Editors

Charles River Editors provides superior editing and original writing services across the digital publishing industry, with the expertise to create digital content for publishers across a vast range of subject matter. In addition to providing original digital content for third party publishers, we also republish civilization's greatest literary works, bringing them to new generations of readers via ebooks.

Sign up here to receive updates about free books as we publish them, and visit Our Kindle Author Page to browse today's free promotions and our most recently published Kindle titles.

Introduction

Tikal's main plaza during the Winter Solstice. Picture by Bjørn Christian Tørrissen.

Tikal

Many ancient civilizations have influenced and inspired people in the 21st century. The Greeks and Romans continue to fascinate the West today. But of all the world's civilizations, none have intrigued people more than the Mayans, whose culture, astronomy, language, and mysterious disappearance all continue to captivate people. In 2012 especially, there was a renewed focus on the Mayans, whose advanced calendar has led many to speculate the world would end on the same date the Mayan calendar ends, but if anything, the focus on the "doomsday" scenario overshadowed the Mayans' true contribution to astronomy, language, sports, and art.

The Maya maintained power in the Yucatan for over a thousand years, and at the height of its "Classical era" (3rd-9th centuries A.D.), the city of Tikal was one of the power centers of the empire. Archaeologists believe Tikal had been built as early as the 5th or 4th century BC, and eventually it became a political, economic and military capital that was an important part of a far-flung network across Mesoamerica, despite the fact it was seemingly conquered by Teotihuacan in the 4th century AD. It seems the foreign rulers came to assimilate Mayan culture, thus ensuring Tikal would continue to be a power base, and as a result, the city would not be abandoned until about the 10th century AD.

As one of the Ancient Maya's most important sites, construction at Tikal was impressive, and even though it was apparently conquered, the city's records were unusually well preserved. This includes a list of the city's dynastic rulers, as well as the tombs and monuments dedicated to them. Thanks to this preservation, Tikal offers researchers their best look at the Ancient Maya and has gone a long way toward helping scholars understand Mayan history.

Tikal: The History of the Ancient Maya's Famous Capital covers the history of the city, as well as the speculation and debate surrounding it. Along with pictures and a bibliography, you will learn about Tikal like you never have before, in no time at all.

Tikal: The History of the Ancient Maya's Famous Capital
About Charles River Editors
Introduction
  A Note on the Periods of Mayan History
  A Note on Pronunciations and Names
  Chapter 1: Early Tikal
  Chapter 2: The First Dynasty
  Chapter 3: The Entrada, Teotihuacán, and the Second Dynasty
  Chapter 4: The Great Hiatus and the Third Dynasty
  Chapter 5: Jasaw Chan K'awiil I and the Fourth Dynasty
  Chapter 6: The Collapse
  Chapter 7: Modern Tikal
  Bibliography

A Note on the Periods of Mayan History

This book follows the traditional system of dividing Mayan history into "periods." Much like European history is divided between the Ancient and Medieval Periods based on whether the Roman Empire had fallen or not, there is a great dividing line in Mayan history called the Classic or Postclassic period.

The apogee of Mayan culture and influence was in the period known to Mesoamerican scholars as the "Classical" period. Ranging from to the 3rd-9th centuries, during this time the region was dominated by two great powers, Tikal and Calakmul, located far to the south of the Yucatán in the northern Highlands. To the west, central Mexico was dominated by the cities of Teotihuacan, Cholula and Monte Albán. This was a period of relative stability, though it probably didn't feel that way as the ruling dynasties of Tikal and Calakmul vied for power and fought numerous proxy wars through their many client states . This period is comparable to the great "cold war" between Athens and Sparta in ancient Greece.

Much like the Roman Empire did not collapse in every area at the same time, the change from the Classic to Postclassic occurred in different places differentially. The Classic Mayan world included a constellation of city-states arranged in great, rival, shifting confederacies. These cities, including the famous centers of Tikal, Palenque, Caracol, and Calakmul, were ruled by kings who were considered semi-divine and were widely commemorated in stone monuments. Eventually, however, the great cities of the Classic Period collapsed, one by one. Far from vanishing, Mayan culture persisted, especially in rural areas, and over time, a new series of cities emerged. While the greatest Classic cities were based in the Highlands of modern Mexico and Guatemala, the Postclassic cities, including Chichén Itzá and Mayapán, emerged in the north in the Yucatan peninsula. Generally speaking, the Postclassic period lasted from the 900s until the arrival of the Spanish in the 1500s.

A Note on Pronunciations and Names

While the Ancient Maya certainly had their own system of writing, the Spanish Conquest ultimately eradicated knowledge of it, so the Mayan languages have been written for almost 500 years using Latin characters adopted from Spanish by missionary priests. Nonetheless, some of the sounds in the Mayan languages do not correspond directly to sounds in English or Spanish, so some guidance is needed for proper pronunciation.

"X" is pronounced as "SH" so the Mayan city of Yaxchilan is pronounced "Ya-sh-i-laan"

"J" is pronounced as a hard "H" so the Mayan name Jasaw is pronounced "Ha-saw"

"Z" is pronounced like an English "S"

"HU" and "UH" are pronounced like a "W" so the Mexican name Teotihuacán is pronounced "Teo-ti-wa-caan"

The Mayan orthography also uses an apostrophe (') to mark a sound that does not appear in most European languages called a glottal stop. This represents a stoppage of air in the throat, a bit like the swallowing of the "TT" in "LITTLE" when pronounced by a Cockney Englishman (which would be written in Mayan orthography as: "li'le"). The glotttal stop is considered to be a consonant.

While the word "Tikal" is Mayan, it is not the name that the Ancient Maya gave to the city when they lived in it. The modern name comes from the Mayan "Ti' ak'al" or "At the Waterhole," a name given by Mayan hunters who traveled through the area and stopped at water reservoirs in the ancient city. The exact name has been lost, but it appears that it was written using a glyph that represented a topknot hair style. Hence, it was probably given the same name, "Mutal." In more formal occasions, it was likely called "Yax Mutal" ("First Topknot"). As a result, some modern archaeologists use the name "Mutal" for talking about the city, but to avoid confusion, this book will stick with the more common name Tikal throughout.[1]

The emblem glyph representing the name Mutal.

As scholars have increasingly learned to read the sophisticated writing system left behind by the Maya, they have gained a more subtle understanding of their naming practices. Generally

---

[1] *Chronicle of the Maya Kings and Queens. Deciphering the Dynasties of the Ancient Maya* by Simon Martin and Nikolai Grube (2000). Thames and Hudson, London. Pg 30

speaking, only the names of kings and queens, as well as a few other individuals, are named in the records, and early archaeologists used names that described the name glyphs, with names like "Stormy Sky," "Curl Snout" or "Great Jaguar Paw." Today it's possible to reconstruct the actual sounds of names like Siyaj Chan K'awiil II, Yax Nuun Ayiin I, or Chak Tok Ich'aak I, but these names are quite long and contain many repetitive elements (much like the continual repetition of the names George and Edward among English kings). This can quickly get confusing for readers, so when this book refers to a king, the Mayan pronunciation will come first, followed by the English glyph names. Subsequent references to the kings will then use the English glyph names to help readers follow along. That said, there are a few exceptions to this due to the growing prominence of the Mayan names for these individuals, most importantly the great king Jasaw Chan K'awiil I.

A jade statue depicting Jasaw Chan K'awiil I

The names of the early kings after Yax Ehb' Xook are largely unimportant to history because of a lack of definitive information about their lives and deeds. One exception is from 317 AD, when there was a break in the male line and the city was ruled by its first recorded woman: queen Lady Une' B'alam ("Baby Jaguar"). This set an important precedent for later claims of succession in the city when usurpers of various shades would look to their own matrilineal ancestors as justification for their place on the throne[2].

---

2 Martin and Grube (2000), Pg 27

Chapter 1: Early Tikal

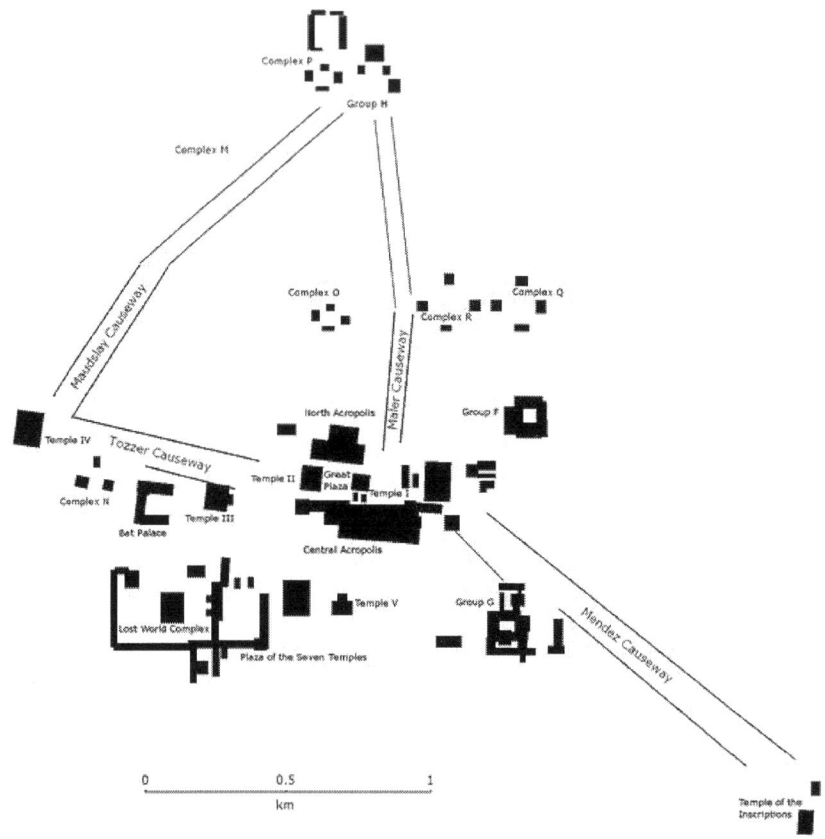

A layout of Tikal

Given how old the city of Tikal is, it's no surprise that the actual origins of the city and the date of its first settlement have been lost to time. In fact, the city was so old that it seems to have predated the Maya's invention of writing, and it was not recorded by later generations, likely because they were more concerned with the founding of the First Dynasty. Thus, the only information historians can glean regarding dates comes from archaeological excavations at the tomb-temple complex of the North Acropolis. The North Acropolis is not only ancient but was sacred and central to the political, religious and social lives of communities for centuries, similar to Westminster Abbey or the Acropolis in Ancient Athens. The Ancient Mayans who lived in Tikal and were unaware of the city's origins itself viewed the North Acropolis not only as ancient but as a symbol of their national identity and sense of self. Thus far, archaeologists have determined that the oldest date for a building at the North Acropolis is about 350 BC, though traces of settlement likely went back centuries before that.[3] By the time the city fell over a millennium later, it had become a complex jumble of construction, a "labyrinth of elevated platforms and walls.[4]"

---

[3] Martin and Grube (2000), Pgs 26 and 43
[4] Exploring Mesoamerica: Places in Time by John M.D. Pohl (1999). Oxford University Press, NY. Pg 70

Pictures of the ruins of the North Acropolis

The city of Tikal was founded in a favorable position along the southern edge of a north-south mountain range that divides the Peten region. Around Tikal, settlers enjoyed a number of varied environments. From the swampy bottomlands called "bajos", they collected crocodiles, frogs, water lilies and logwood trees. Along the hills, they raised corn and other crops and navigated the river valleys as trade routes, bringing up useful items like shells, seaweed and stingray spines from the coast of what is today Belize[5]. The city that they founded would eventually become the longest-inhabited Classical center, with an estimated 39 recorded rulers.

It appears that the early inhabitants of Tikal worshiped "spirit forces personified by [a] giant birdlike stucco mask.[6]" These masks have been found in the temples of the North Acropolis, and archaeologists have uncovered similar monuments in other contemporary Lowland Pre-Classic cities like El Mirador, Nakbé, Cerros and Uaxactun. There is no consensus on exactly what god or goddess was represented by the masks, but there are two potential candidates based on

---

5 *The Lords of Tikal: Rulers of An Ancient Maya City* by Peter D. Harrison (1999) by Thames and Hudson, London. Pgs 45-47.
6 Pohl (1999) pg 70

documents that survived the Spanish and records kept by the Spanish themselves. In the Highland mythological text *Popoh Vuh*, there is one candidate called "Vucub Caquix," a lord of twilight who dominated the earth before he was displaced by the hero twins Hunahpu and Xbalanque. Another possibility is the creator god Itzamna, who was recorded as being revered by the Maya of the Yucatec peninsula by the Franciscan priest Diego de Landa. The interpretation of the North Acropolis monuments and the surrounding temples varies greatly depending on whether this figure is a dark lord of the era before humans or a beloved creator. Of course, it is also possible that this deity, who was worshiped in a period of great antiquity, was displaced by the emergence of later gods like Tlaloc or Quetzalcoatl. Regardless, there are no known written accounts of this deity's name.

Once it emerged as a political unit worthy of mention, early Tikal was dominated by two sister-cities located roughly 20 miles (32 km) to the northwest. These were El Mirador and Nakbé, cities which adopted an elaborate Mesoamerican urban tradition from groups like the Olmecs further north. This included stone buildings, temples on top of pyramids, the ball game,[7] and the construction of stone monuments. The most important of these monuments to emerge out of the El Mirador/Nakbé tradition were "stelae" (the plural of "stela"), which were large stone slabs covered in elaborate carvings commemorating important events. Similar to royal inscriptions in ancient Egypt, kings in Tikal would erect these stelae to commemorate great victories, important calendric events (the equivalent of decades and centenaries), investitures of power, and deaths. Since little of the early Mayan writing has survived the ravages of time and the Spanish Conquest, these stelae are often important sources of information about what the kings wanted observers to know about themselves[8].

---

7 A sport that combined game with ritual, involving stone courts and players who attempted to knock rubber balls through stone hoops without the use of their hands.
8 Pohl (1999) pgs 68-70

Picture of a stela in Tikal

The ballgame court at Tikal. Picture by Simon Burchell.

Chapter 2: The First Dynasty

By 300 AD, the El Mirador/Nakbé political entity was crumbling, so its various vassal states were able to act independently, including not only Tikal but other major players of later history like Uaxactun and Calakmul. In this vacuum of power emerged what anthropologists call "chiefdoms," relatively simple units ruled by a single leader (the chief) and his personal bodyguard who is able to extract tribute from surrounding farmers. Chiefs might in turn send tribute up the line to a larger, paramount chief who controlled a number of lesser chiefdoms[9].

It was out of this relatively chaotic and occasionally brutal situation that Tikal's leadership began to consolidate local power, and eventually the rulers established a system to transfer power from one generation to the next. They also created basic bureaucratic institutions, such as a priesthood, which gave further continuity and regularity to government. During this process, they undoubtedly looked to the examples of El Mirador and Nakbé, as well as other neighboring cities. In time, what emerged was the creation of the First Dynasty.

The early information about the First Dynasty is largely unavailable because much of it was destroyed via the elimination of the city's early monuments in 378 AD, but even if they had survived, the records would have been spotty because of the lack of sophistication in Mayan writing at the time. It would be some time before the people of Tikal themselves were involved in perfecting writing; in fact, contemporary records were only kept starting around 292 AD, so everything that scholars can piece together about the earlier eras of the First Dynasty have come from what was written by subsequent generations of Tikal's residents after the fact.[10]

As a result, scholars' estimates of the dates of the reigns of the early monarchs are based upon a technique called average reign length estimates. Simon Martin, a historian of the region, compiled all of the known start and end dates for the reigns of Mayan kings and queens and created an average of 22.5 years. He was then able to put them onto undated lists of kings, such as those available for early Tikal[11]. While this system obviously does not always (or even most of the time) provide the correct date, it offers up the best technique for dating events like the founding of the First Dynasty.

At the same time, knowledge of those early days has improved over the last few decades as historians unearth new information about the First Dynasty. For example, scholars long thought that Great Jaguar Paw, the last ruler of the dynasty, was the 9th in his line, but recent findings have uncovered the names of four more early kings. When added to the average reign length technique, this pushes back the reign of Yax Ehb' Xook (First Step Shark) to roughly 90 AD and opens up the possibility that his remains are those found in a splendid, sumptuous tomb called Burial 85 at the North Acropolis[12].

What is clear is that royal life in early Tikal centered around the Great Plaza, a broad paved area between the North Acropolis temple-tombs and the Central Acropolis, a complex structure that included administrative facilities, courts of law, and administrative areas. It was in splendor here that the First Dynasty constructed their empire. Other elite families tended to have their own homes scattered around the neighboring hills and farms, where they could control the local population[13].

---

10 Martin and Grube (2000), Pg 26
11 "The Painted King List: A Commentary on Codex-Style Dynastic Vases." by Simon Martin in *The Maya Vase Book: A Corpus of Rollout Photographs of Maya Vases by Justin Kerr, Volume 5,* edited by Barbara Kerr and Justin Kerr, pp. 847-867. Kerr Associates, New York.
12 Martin and Grube (2000), Pgs 26-27
13 Harrison (1999) pgs 73-75

Royal residences in Tikal. Picture by Dennis Jarvis.

Temple I with the North Acropolis to the left and Center Acropolis to the right.

One definitive element of the political life of the First Dynasty was the city's conflict with its primary political rival, the nearby city of Uaxactun. In many ways, Uaxactun remains in the record as a ghostly twin, mostly because its eventual conquest by Tikal meant that its early history was erased and that it remained in Tikal's shadow after that. However, it seems that early Uaxactun was nearly equal in power, making the two legitimate rivals. Like Tikal, Uaxactun emerged out of the chaos of the collapse of the old Nakbé and El Mirador power structure, but the eventual conquest of Uaxactun by the Second Dynasty after the Teotihuacano Entrada would solidify the city of Tikal as the dominant power in the region[14].

The last king of the First Dynasty was one of the most important. Chak Tok Ich'aak I, whose name is written as either Great Burning Paw or (more commonly) Great Jaguar Paw, came to the throne around roughly 360 AD, and it was during his reign that the city began to look outward in a much greater way than before. Much of this outward looking perspective involved the importation of goods and ideas from Central Mexico, specifically Teotihuacán; trade had existed for some time, but it reached new levels of sophistication during this period, especially involving

---

14 Pohl (1999) pg 72

high quality ceramics. As discussed further below, Great Jaguar Paw may have written his own death warrant, because it seems that the Teotihuacano army traveled along these same trade routes to come kill him. Another direct impact of this contact was the creation of the Lost World Complex[15].

Perhaps the most important construction during the rule of the First Dynasty was a complex of temples and support buildings poetically called the Mundo Perdido (or "Lost World"). Located at the western edge of the city center, it was the largest temple complex in the Preclassical city, dominated by a large four-sided pyramid topped with three temples, some of which may have been used as solar observatories to chart solstices and equinoxes. The architectural impact of the Mexican contact on the Lost World complex can be seen as early as 250 AD, long before Great Jaguar Paw's trade contacts[16].

One of the more important elements of the Lost World's architectural style is that it was the first area of Tikal to utilize a style called "Talud-Tablero." Unlike an Egyptian pyramid with four smooth sides, Mesoamerican pyramids were built like layer cakes or steps, with ever-smaller square blocks placed on top of one another. The Talud-Tablero style, also called the "slop and panel" style, is characterized by "pairs of taludes [sloped layers] and framed tableros [horizontal layers] that pass completely around a platform , and stairs flanked by balustrades that are capped with finial blocks (called *remates*)."[17] This is important because the style originated not amongst the Maya but in the mighty Central Mexican city of Teotihuacán. The interaction between Tikal and this distant imperial capital would come to dominate Tikal's political fortunes in the coming years, but the Lost World also shows the importance of Mexican styles at an early date in Tikal.

---

[15] Martin and Grube (2000), pg 28
[16] *Ibid*
[17] "Architectural Aspects of Interaction between Tikal and Teotihuacan" by Juan Pedro Laporte in *The Maya and Teotihuacan: Reinterpreting Early Classic Interaction* (2003) by Geoffrey E. Braswell (ed.). University of Austin Press. pg 200

One of the Lost World pyramids. Picture by Dennis Jarvis.

A Lost World Temple. Picture by Mike Murga.

The roof of Temple III.

A step pyramid that's part of "Complex Q" in Tikal.

Chapter 3: The Entrada, Teotihuacán, and the Second Dynasty

The destiny of Tikal was forever changed on January 31st, 378 AD when a massive army arrived at the city's gates. This event has become known by the Spanish name "Entrada" which means simply the "Entry," as in "the entry of Teotihuacán". While there is no clear record of the events due to the sheer scale of destruction that took place, it's clear neither Tikal nor the Maya as a whole had ever seen anything like it because these foreign soldiers not only conquered but also subsequently ruled Tikal despite the fact they had come from Teotihuacán in Central Mexico, about 630 miles (1013 kilometers) away.[18] In short order, the Teotihuacanos dispatched the rulers of Tikal and installed their own people to rule, which ironically resulted in positioning Tikal as the largest and most important city in the Mayan lands. In the process, the Teotihuacanos not only changed Tikal but the direction of the Mayan civilization for centuries to come.

This conquest came about after trade contacts were established between the Mayan regions and

---

18 Martin and Grube (2000), Pgs 29

what is today Central Mexico. These contacts went back centuries and included the transfer of not only goods but also ideas. An early example of this was the Talud-Tablero architecture found in the Lost World Complex of Tikal, and another clearly identifiable Mexican import found in early Tikal is green-hued obsidian, which can be clearly identified to sites in Mexico[19].

Early contacts between the Teotihuacanos and the Maya of Tikal and other cities began in the western Mayan city of Kaminaljuyu, which became wealthy acting as a go-between for the two peoples[20]. Tikal's trade was primarily with the city of Teotihuacán, which was located in the Valley of Mexico near today's Mexico City. Thriving between 100-750 AD, this was one of the largest cities in the ancient world, with a population of at least 200,000. In comparison, when Tikal was at the height of its power in the 8th century, it had a population of around 60,000. Teotihuacán was a supremely well-planned and efficient city that was able to field massive armies and extend its power far beyond its home base to create a unified empire of the type that was never possible in the less fertile Mayan lands[21].

The ruins of Teotihuacán

---

19 *Ibid*
20 "Understanding Early Classic Interaction Between Kaminaljuyu and Central Mexico" by Geoffrey E. Braswell in *The Maya and Teotihuacan: Reinterpreting Early Classic Interaction* (2003) by Geoffrey E. Braswell (ed.). University of Austin Press. pgs 105-142
21 Pohl (1999) pgs 53-66

There is a long-standing debate over exactly how much influence Teotihuacán (and Central Mexico in general) had over the development of the Mayan heartland. Mayanists have long been protective of their region and have tended to downplay Mexican influence and emphasize Mayan creativity. Before the decipherment of the Mayan script, they argued that Mayan leaders emulated styles from Teotihuacán but had no direct contact or rule[22]. In this interpretation, what happened in 378 was that Great Jaguar Paw, who had initiated trade with Teotihuacán, died and was replaced by his son, Lord Curl Snout, who formalized the trade relationship and began a period of stylistic emulation of their trade partners[23]. However, over time, archaeologists and historians have found evidence that the transfer of power in 378 from Great Jaguar Paw to Curl Snout - while it may have been inspired by earlier trade contacts - was anything but peaceful.

Today, there is a general consensus that Tikal was conquered by a mighty army, and the rumors of the conquering army's march must have preceded it, as such a force could not move quickly without horses (which arrived with the Europeans). The first record historians have of its movements comes from a smaller city called El Perú, roughly 49 miles (78 kilometers) to the west of Tikal. El Perú fell on January 23rd, and the armies arrived at Tikal eight days later after traveling up the San Pedro Martir River.[24]

At the head of this army was a figure called Siyaj K'ak' ("Fire Born"), who appears to have been a general. The surviving writing says that Siyaj K'ak' was sent at the head of the army at the behest of a mysterious figure called "Spearthrower Owl." This name is not written out using Mayan script but is instead an image of an owl bearing an atlatl (a device for throwing spears). The owl may have been a symbol of a warrior god or caste in the city, but the name "Spearthrower Owl" appears more likely to be a title than the actual name of the person. Traditionally, Spearthrower Owl has been thought of as the ruler of Teotihuacán who sponsored the expedition, based on some monuments that appear to place the date of his ascension to a throne (which throne is not certain, but it's not Tikal's) on May 4th, 374 and his death on June 10th, 439. The records also suggest he took a Mayan wife[25]. However, recently there has been a debate over whether the title actually refers to a god, because some murals found at Teotihuacán refer to a site called "Spearthrower Owl Hill", and these murals are roughly contemporaneous with the Entrada of 378. In this understanding, Spearthrower Owl is a martial god similar to the later Aztec god Huitzilopochtli. The archaeologists and historians will have to find further evidence (including a search for Spearthrower Owl Hill) before a more definitive statement on the subject can be made.[26]

Either way, when this army arrived, the Maya likely resisted, but Tikal had no walls, a

---

22 "Forward" in *The Maya and Teotihuacan: Reinterpreting Early Classic Interaction* (2003) by Geoffrey E. Braswell (ed.). University of Austin Press. pgs xiii-xvi
23 Pohl (1999) pg 72
24 Martin and Grube (2000), Pg 29
25 Martin and Grube (2000), Pg 30
26 "Spearthrower Owl Hill. A Toponym at Atatelco, Teotihuacan" by Jesper Nielsen and Christopher Helmke (2008) in the journal *Latin American Antiquity* 19(4), pgs. 459-171.

defensive feature that would not appear in Mayan cities until centuries later. It also seems that the resistance didn't do much harm to the armies of Teotihuacán, which quickly conquered other cities as well. Images found on pottery depict the arrival of the Mexican warriors and ambassadors and the death of Great Jaguar Paw on January 31st, 378. More direct evidence of conquest comes from Uaxactun, where a mural image depicts a submissive Maya and a dominant Teotihuacano from the time period[27]. It is useful to compare this image to the type of imagery found at the city of Chichén Itzá some 600 years later. There is a similar debate at Chichén about a possible invasion by a Central Mexican power (this time the Toltec Empire), but there is no record there of conquest and no images of Mayans dominated by Mexicans[28].

There is also archaeological evidence for a change in the nature of the Mexican-Mayan contact at this point as well. For example, Tikal became home to considerably more Teotihuacano objects after 378, especially lidded tripods coated in painted stucco. Even more notable is the fact that there was a systematic destruction of monuments from before 378, and the use of the broken stone as either fill for new construction projects or their exportation to other, less important cities. For a royal system whose legitimacy was founded upon a connection to the past (especially in the form of the tombs of the North Acropolis), the destruction of these past records indicate a major political break occurred on that year[29].

---

[27] *Ibid*
[28] A copy of the image can be found on the Website of the Museo Popol Vuh of the Universidad Francisco Marroquin, accessed online at: http://www.popolvuh.ufm.edu/exhibiciones/u-wach-ulew/uwach05.htm
[29] Martin and Grube (2000), Pg 30

A stucco mask adorning a temple in the North Acropolis. Picture by Bjørn Christian Tørrissen.

It's also known that during the same year, an army out of Tikal finally conquered Uaxactun and eliminated its ruling line. In its place, the brother of the lord of Tikal, a man named Lord Smoking Frog, was put on the throne and founded his own cadet dynasty that would rule in the shadow of Tikal[30]. The last date scholars have for the fall of a surrounding city was 381. The Teotihuacanos would put up their own dynasties at all of these sites, but it's unclear what the relationship between Tikal and these other conquests was, or if there was an effective central coordination. If there was, it would eventually break down in the wars that would emerge a few generations later[31].

Regardless of whether Spearthrower Owl was a man or a god, he was not the titular ruler of Tikal for long, because the record suggests that his son, Yax Nuun Ayiin I ("Curl Snout") took the throne on September 12, 379. This date marks the beginning of the Second Dynasty, and Curl Snout would reign for 25 years until his death on June 17, 404. When he came to the throne,

---

30 Pohl (1999) pg 71
31 Martin and Grube (2000), pg 30

Curl Snout was only a boy, and it appears that the general Siyaj held the reins of power as a regent over the city during Curl Snout's youth.

A stela at Tikal that depicts Curl Snout. Picture by H. Grobe.

While Curl Snout would not live to a ripe old age (if Spearthrower Owl was a man, he apparently outlived his son by 35 years), his reign was notable as the high watermark of Teotihucano imperialism in the region. This was when the monuments dating before 378 were destroyed, and the regime aimed to re-create the royal imagery of Central Mexico in its monuments and murals. This first generation of conquerors had no connections to the land they ruled and derived their legitimacy from their distant patron Spearthrower Owl, but Curl Snout did marry a wife with Mayan royal titles, so there was at least a nominal attempt to associate the Second Dynasty with the previous power structure.[32] It is believed that Curl Snout was buried in the magnificent Burial 10 in Temple 34, which was the first building to break out of the traditional front face of the North Acropolis (though others would follow in later generations)[33].

Upon Curl Snout's death, his heir was not yet considered an adult, so just as Siyaj K'ak' ruled as a regent during Curl Snout's youth, another non-royal by the name of Siyaj Chan K'inich ("Sky Born Sun God") would rule from 406-411. After sitting under the thumb of the regent Siyaj Chan K'inich for five years, the new king, Siyaj Chan K'awiil II (Lord Stormy Sky), ascended to the throne of Tikal on November 26, 411. He would have a particularly long and productive reign before he died on February 3, 456 (45 years, twice the average).

---

32 Martin and Grube (2000), Pgs 32-33
33 Ibid

A stela depicting Stormy Sky

The reign of Lord Stormy Sky was characterized by a re-emergence of Mayan imagery in royal propaganda and an emphasis on the continuity of the Second Dynasty with the royalty of the First Dynasty through his mother's line. This was a distinct break with the imagery of his father's reign, which depicted the Maya only as subservient and was dominated by imported Mexican symbols. In fact, there was a conscious use of archaisms in the art; for instance, artisans basically re-created a 150 year old stela with only slightly different wording. The words of other monuments also placed an emphasis on the precedence of royal blood being transferred via the female line in the case of the 4th century queen, Lady Une' B'alam[34]. Furthermore, emphasis was taken off of ritual at the consciously Mexican Lost World complex and returned to the thoroughly Mayan North Acropolis. Other evidence of the change is that the royal regalia depicted in the stelae returned to the traditional Maya form created in the 3rd century, and this would remain basically unchanged until the collapse of the city. Even the king's name - possibly a regnal name[35] - was a reference to an earlier king, Stormy Sky, who ascended to the throne around 307 AD[36].

What inspired the triumphant Teotihuacanos to "nativize" and emphasize the Mayan culture and dynastic tradition that they had previously scorned? The written and archaeological records are mostly silent on this, but it's possible to make comparisons to similar cases around the world where an invading warrior elite conquers a wide swath of territory. Examples would include the French Normans in Britain, the Hellenic Greeks in much of their post-Alexander empire, the Turkic Safavid Dynasty in Persia, and the Manchus in China. In all of these cases, the elite established not only a dominant dynasty but also installed smaller lines throughout the new territory, and in the process, they spread themselves quite thin. The conquering Teotihuacanos must have needed to learn to speak the local language to communicate not only with the peasantry but with Tikal's local administrators and bureaucrats, and over time, subsequent generations of the elite who grew up communicating with the locals likely had no direct experience or emotional ties to their native homeland. Moreover, they may have resented having to send tribute back "home" and may have further assimilated in efforts to legitimize themselves to avoid local uprisings.

One long-term effect of this period of strength, during which Tikal-Teotihuacán influence spread throughout the Mayan Lowlands, was a reinforcement of the dynastic system. In fact, while Tikal had been an early pioneer in this form of governance, it was only with the influence of Teotihuacán's Mexican tradition that it reached its peak. Tikal's dominance also helped spread the cult of the rain god Tlaloc (who became known by the Mayan name Chaak) throughout the Mayan lands, where he displaced the earlier bird-faced deity as the principal god[37]. There has

---

34 Martin and Grube (2000), Pg 34; Mesoamerica 72
35 A name chosen by a king or other ruler at the time of his or her ascension. A modern example would be the names of popes, so Jorge Mario Bergoglio became Pope Francis I.
36 "Tikal's Dynastic Rulers" accessed online at: http://www.tikalpark.com/dynasty.htm

been some argument that this dynastic and religious tradition fostered opposition amongst more conservative Mayan groups and helped garner support for Tikal's enemies in traditionalist Calakmul, which claimed royal descent from El Mirador.

A Classical era depiction of Chaak

Chapter 4: The Great Hiatus and the Third Dynasty

As archaeologists began to piece together Tikal's history in the mid-20th century, they encountered a confusing problem. Between 562 and 692 - a full 130 years - not a single dated monument was built in the city, nor were there any large construction projects. It was as if the leadership of the city had simply left for over a century. Further complicating this picture is the fact that many Early Classic monuments that predate 550 AD were vandalized[38]. This time became known as the "Hiatus", but today, scholars have a much richer understanding of this period. The lack of monuments at Tikal during the Hiatus no longer hinders an understanding of the period as much as it previously did because much has been learned from decorated commemorative ceramics and monuments in other cities.

Far from being a period of quiescence, it is now known that this period was marked by chaos, political intrigue, and war. The roots of the Hiatus begin in a troubled period between 508 and

---

37 Martin and Grube (2000), Pg 35
38 Pohl (1999) pg 71

562. After the death of Chak Tok Ich'aak on July 24, 508, there appears to have been a vacuum of power, which was made perfectly clear 13 days later when the relatively weak city of Yaxchilan captured one of Tikal's vassal cities. The exact events after this are largely lost because most of the stelae are defaced or unfinished, but it appears that Tikal's elite became divided between two factions.

Around this time, a figure called the "Lady of Tikal" appeared on the stage. A daughter of Chak Tok Ich'aak, she was only four years old when her father died and was undoubtedly a pawn of a larger faction, at least initially. She appears on stelae in 511, 514, and 527, but always in association with a male co-ruler, and in 527, she was depicted as ruling alongside Kaloomte' B'alam, a general involved in the 486 attack on the city of Maasal and usually considered the 19th king of Tikal. However, somewhere between 527 and 537, she becomes associated with the 20th king, lord "Bird Claw."

By 557, fortunes appear to have shifted, as another king, "Double Bird", is marked as the 21st king. Double Bird was also the child of Chak Tok Ich'aak II, born in January 508, only seven months before his father's death. He is commemorated as having come to power on January 29, 537, and the monuments record him as having "returned" (presumably from exile) during this period.[39]

As these records suggest, the death of Chak Tok Ich'aak II led to dynastic strife, with different elements of his court seizing his two young children as pawns to make separate claims to the throne. Meanwhile, the internal divisions of the city meant that Tikal' elites were unable to maintain their control on wider Mayan politics. In 553, Double Bird is recorded as sponsoring the ruler in distant Caracol, but in the same year, the far closer kingdom of Naranjo became a vassal of the rival city of Calakmul. This was followed in 556 by a direct war with the now-rebellious Caracol, where Tikal lost a vassal to the upstart city. Finally, in 562 there was an event called a "star war", a war that was timed to coincide with the movements of Venus. During this war, an army likely consisting of the combined forces of Caracol and Calakmul overran Tikal and ritually killed Double Bird.

It's certainly noteworthy that early archaeological studies have documented the simultaneous collapses of Teotihuacán and Tikal, but it's unclear how or whether the two are linked. Did Teotihuacán recall its soldiers from Tikal? Was the fall of Teotihuacán seen as a withdrawal of divine mandate and something that might have galvanized Tikal's enemies? Another theory is that the collapse was brought about by the collapse of trade and the inability of Tikal's elites to maintain their own trade routes. Regardless of exactly what the connections were between the collapse of Tikal and Teotihuacán, 562 AD was a momentous one in Mesoamerica because it witnessed the collapse of the region's mightiest city and the conquest and subjugation of its second-most powerful.

---

39 Martin and Grube (2000), Pg 39

Debates over the internal divisions in Tikal and the effects of the collapse of Teotihuacán also overshadow the fact that the collapse of Tikal's hegemony was at least partly a product of a geopolitical strategy by two rivals: Caracol and, especially, Calakmul. Calakmul was, like Tikal, an inheritor of the ancient Preclassic era, having emerged from being a vassal of El Mirador and Nakbé. The capital of the kingdom was located 24 miles (39 km) to the north of the ruins of old El Mirador and seemed to have claimed to be the rightful heir of that ancient city. In this way, the rulers of Calakmul leapfrogged over Tikal and Teotihuacán, effectively asserting themselves as the true heirs of the Mayan civilization.

Calakmul and the kingdom it ruled, called Kaan (the Kingdom of the Snake), remained in the shadow of Tikal during Tikal's glory days, but the kingdom was never conquered by Tikal or the Teotihuacanos. In the 540s, Calakmul began to cement power and began implementing a strategy to displace Tikal. King Stone Hand Jaguar and then King Sky Witness worked throughout the 540s and 550s to bring to heel one small city after another in order to create a ring of enemies around Tikal. In the process, they apparently hoped to be able to starve Tikal politically by denying it tribute from vassals and preventing it from reconstituting trade networks to Central Mexico that were in decline with the collapse of Teotihuacán.

It appears that despite their divisions, the Tikal elites were aware of this strategy, at least after Sky Witness' troops brought Caracol under his banner in 561[40]. Tikal's last Second Dynasty king, Lord Double Bird, ordered an attack on Caracol in 562, no doubt hoping to break the stranglehold that Calakmul had created. Unfortunately, he underestimated the strength of his enemies or perhaps overestimated his own power. He not only failed to take Caracol in that attack but subsequently lost everything in the alliance's counterattack[41].

Sometime around 593 AD, a new king is recorded as ascending to the throne of Tikal: King Animal Skull, 22nd in the line. There is evidence to show that this ascension involved the rise of a third dynasty to power. For one, there is an oblique reference to the ritual killing of Double Bird, and the pottery made for Animal Skull makes much of his matrilineal connections to Tikal's elite but is completely silent about his father. In fact, scholars' understanding of the line of the earliest kings comes from retrospective ceramics that trace his lineage. Both of these elements give weight to the argument that Animal Skull was part of a new ruling family put into power by the victorious Caracol and Calakmul, a common occurrence in Mayan conquests[42].

In the normal course of events, this conquest should have been the political end of Tikal. A typical example would be Tikal's old rival Uaxactun, which became a minor player after its conquest. There's no doubt that the victorious powers of Caracol and Calakmul had much at stake in keeping Tikal under their thumb.

---

40 Martin and Grube (2000), Pg 104
41 Puhl (1999) pg 74
42 Martin and Grube (2000), Pg 40-42

After the death of Animal Skull in 628 AD, there appears to have been a relatively orderly transition, as his tomb was constructed immediately and was well made and adorned. However, this unity was not to last, as a schism appears to have occurred as early as 648 AD. Roughly 70 miles (112 kilometers) to the southwest of Tikal, a new city named Dos Pilas had a king, B'alaj Chan K'awiil, who claimed to be the legitimate ruler of Tikal. His ascension to the throne was backed by Calakmul[43], but meanwhile, back in Tikal, a ruler named Nuun Ujol Chaak ("Shield Skull") - a rival of B'alaj Chan K'awiil in Dos Pilas - took the throne.

In response, Yuknoom the Great of Calakmul launched another star war in 657 to eject the upstart, but the results of this conflict are confusing. Shield Skull fled Tikal to the distant city of Palenque (another enemy of Calakmul), but B'alaj Chan K'awiil and the Dos Pilas elites seemingly did not return in triumph to Tikal. It's unclear why this happened, but some have speculated that Calakmul decided to rule the city directly. Shield Skull is recorded as being present in Palenque in 659, but he eventually retook Tikal and then Dos Pilas itself in 672. Yet again, Calakmul attacked Shield Skull's forces and drove him out of Dos Pilas in 677, and he was defeated once and for all in 679 AD[44]. While scholars aren't certain, it seems that the Third Dynasty continued in exile in Dos Pilas until around 807 AD.

To understand Tikal during the Hiatus, one helpful comparison is 20th century China. Internally divided and beset by enemies, the traditional dynasty (the Second Dynasty in Tikal or the Manchus in China) was overthrown and puppet rulers - perhaps with ideological ties to foreign powers - are put into place (Tikal's Third Dynasty and the pro-Western government of Chiang Kai Shek), and the nation is ringed with enemy states (Naranjo, Caracol and others for Tikal and Japan, Korea and India for China). When revolution topples the government, a rump of survivors flees and establishes a petty domain under the protection of the former masters, for whom it is useful to recognize the exiles as the legitimate government (in these cases, Dos Pilas and Taiwan).

Despite his overall failure to restore Tikal to glory, Shield Skull was successful in igniting the embers of his city's independence and power, something his son was to see through. This son, Jasaw Chan K'awiil I, was possibly the most important ruler in the long history of Tikal.

.

---

43 Martin and Grube (2000), Pg 42
44 Martin and Grube (2000), Pgs 42, 57

An altar depicting Jasaw Chan K'awiil I

Chapter 5: Jasaw Chan K'awiil I and the Fourth Dynasty

The most famous building at Tikal, and arguably one of the most famous and evocative buildings in all of the Mayan kingdoms, is the plainly named Temple I. Temple I, which stands 154 feet (47 meters), is not the tallest building at the site, but its incredibly steep sides, crowning temple, and the existence of its mirror in Temple II across the plaza all give it a remarkable quality that visitors have noted for centuries. The tomb sits hard against the North Acropolis, but it is not properly part of that complex; in essence, Temples I and II dramatically frame the Acropolis. It is perhaps fitting that the tomb of Jasaw Chan K'awiil I - the greatest king of Tikal

– both gives a nod to the burial traditions of the North Acropolis but also breaks them, because after Jasaw, no other king would be buried in the ancient halls of their ancestors.

The back of Temple I

The front of Temple I. Picture by Dennis Jarvis.

Jasaw Chan K'awiil faced an uphill battle when he came to power on May 3, 682. He viewed himself as a restorer of Tikal, but he probably had little to work with: his father's armies had been defeated five years earlier, a rival dynasty claimed his throne in Dos Pilas, and it is possible that enemies occupied his capital city. While he may have had some help from his father's allies in Palenque, the fact that he overcame all of these challenges and finally defeated the armies of Calakmul in open battle on August 5, 695 is a testament to his skill as an administrator, diplomat and tactician[45].

---

45 Martin and Grube (2000), Pg 44

As a restorer, Jasaw Chan K'awiil sought to remind his city of its former glories, so he openly revived the symbolism of long-fallen Teotihuacán, especially its regalia (much in the same way that Europeans would use Roman symbolism centuries after that empire's collapse). He had an eye for the past, including hosting the commemoration of his 695 battle on September 14 in order to also commemorate the 13th K'atun anniversary (256 years - an auspicious number) of the death of his Teotihuacano progenitor Spearthrower Owl[46].

After breaking the stranglehold of Calakmul's noose around Tikal, Jasaw Chan K'awiil began to recreate the old empire. He may have taken Masaal and Naranjo as the spoils of the 695 victory (though he had to put down rebellions in Naranjo later), and he must have taken great satisfaction in sacking Dos Pilas in 705. By 711, he had retaken the cities of Motul de San José, El Perú and Uaxactun. Once these conquests were complete and the Noose was broken, Jasaw Chan K'awiil set about a large number of building projects in the capital before his death in 731 AD.

Despite his emphasis on continuity with the ancient past and his obvious assertions of the inheritance of Teotihuacán's legitimacy, Jasaw Chan K'awiil appears to have been the founder of the Fourth (and final) Dynasty at Tikal. Of course, historians don't know (and probably never will) whether Jasaw Chan K'awiil was actually the direct inheritor of Double Bird, the last Second Dynasty ruler, but either way, he was succeeded by several generations of rulers. His son Yik'in Chan K'awiil, the 27th king, ascended in 734 and built upon his father's triumphs to strengthen the empire, forever shattering Calakmul's desire to dominate in a series of military campaigns that also reshaped the center of Tikal and reflected its return to grandeur.

At the city's height around this time, it had over 60,000 inhabitants covering 10 square miles (25 square kilometers)[47]. This period of strength continued through two more kings until the reign of Yax Nuun Ayiin II in 794 AD. During the city's peak, its merchants were trading in, salt, cotton, cacao, obsidian, jade, and feathers, and the city dominated the region's rivers and ports, reconstituting trade networks that had declined during the Hiatus.[48]

Chapter 6: The Collapse

At the start of the 9th century, it may have seemed to Tikal's residents that the city had passed its darkest days and would rule the region for another six centuries, but in reality, the city and its sociopolitical order would soon be history. This period would become famously known as the Mayan Collapse.

After the relative prosperity of Yax Nuun Ayiin, the Tikal elites once again went quiet. The important ritual date of the 10th Bak'tun in 830 was not commemorated in stone, one part of a 60 year period known as the Second Hiatus during which there were no monuments. Between the

---
46 Martin and Grube (2000), Pg 45
47 Pohl (1999) pg 68
48 Pohl (1999) pg 73

years of 809 and 869, there is no evidence of any central authority in the city; while there must have been some form of order, there is nothing to suggest that it was a traditional dynasty with pretensions to the classic power.

In 869, Jasaw Chan K'awiil II, a name likely chosen in homage to the famous king of the past, had a stela erected in his honor as king of Tikal, but he was unable to prevent rulers in Tikal's small vassal cities from asserting their claims to Tikal's throne, something that had never occurred before. The last monument built in the city was in 889 AD, and while the city was not immediately abandoned (there is archaeological evidence of settlements there lasting until the late 10th or early 11th centuries), the subsequent generations of residents did not even maintain the pretence of dynastic rule. In fact, some of the residents actually squatted in the palaces and temples and mined the North Acropolis tombs for their treasures. Similarly, in Dos Pilas, crude earthworks were built that cut right across old roads, courtyards and even buildings[49]. There is also evidence that local groups in the region regularly raided each other.

One of the palaces in Tikal. Picture by Dennis Jarvis.

The Mayan Collapse has fascinated Westerners since the ruins were first discovered and described by 19th century European visitors. The modern-day obsession with "mysterious sites,"

---

[49] Martin and Grube (2000), Pg 33

evidenced by a raft of dubious documentaries and spurious scholarship attributing Mayan triumphs to everyone from aliens to Atlantis, has obscured the fact that recent scholarship has done much to clear up not only the details of the dynastic struggles of the Maya but also the reasons for the eventual collapse of their civilization. In fact, there is nothing shocking about the idea that an entire cultural area can suffer an irretrievable collapse, as history offers plenty of examples. In his book on the subject, *Collapse, How Societies Choose to Fail or Succeed*, Jared Diamond examined not only the Maya but also Easter Island, the Pitcairn Islands, the Anasazi, the Vikings in Greenland, and contemporary China, Australia and Hispaniola.

In his book, Diamond argues that the Mayan Collapse was a gradual ecological development brought about by the political and economic systems of Tikal and other cities. Mayan agriculture was heavily dependent upon corn, a relatively protein-poor food (compared to wheat and barley), and they lacked access to a wide selection of domesticated animals, since they only had access to dogs and turkeys. This production was significantly lower in the Maya area than in other parts of Mesoamerica because of poor soils and humid climate. Humidity prevented storing corn for more than a season, the lack of draft animals meant that food could not be transported long distances, and agriculture was labor intensive[50].

As the population levels peaked in the Late Classic period, the time of Tikal's second zenith around the 700s, Mayan farmers were exploiting increasingly precarious farmlands, leading to deforestation and erosion on an unprecedented scale. Even the glorious buildings in the center of Tikal would have needed immense amounts of wood to make the thick layers of plaster that covered the surfaces. In turn, this may have led to human-produced droughts caused by the disruptions to water cycles, all due to lack of forests and the speed of runoff without the entrapment caused by roots. Furthermore, in 760 AD, the worst regional drought in thousands of years began, lasting over four decades and exacerbating all of these problems As eroded farmland was abandoned and drought spread, there would have been increasing conflicts amongst farmers and growing anger at the ruling class that was not performing its role as intercessors with the divine. In fact, in the city of Copán, that anger would turn to outright violence; the royal palace was burned to the ground in 850 AD, and nothing was heard from the elites after that.[51]

The Collapse affected a wide range of Classical cities, including Tikal, Calakmul, Palenque and Caracol, but it did not affect all of the Maya. This was especially true of those in the far north of the Yucatan Peninsula, who would found new cities like Uxmal, Chichén Itzá and Mayapán in the wake of the Collapse. Moreover, the Maya themselves around Tikal did not disappear. In fact, they live there still, making up the majority of the population of northern Guatemala and surrounding Mexican states. Instead, the Collapse should be understood as a political event: the collapse of the traditional Mayan dynastic system and the loss of much of the

---

50 *Collapse: How Societies Choose to Fail or Succeed* (2005) by Jared Diamond. Pgs 164-5
51 *ibid* pgs 169-170

Mayan population in the resulting famines.

What did the Collapse look like? It was a slow-moving event, affecting peripheral areas first and the great heartlands later. Famine and drought would have driven peasants from marginal lands, filling the cities with beggars and swelling recruits to armies. Some families would march far away to the north in search of new lands, founding Yucatecan cities like Uxmal. At the same time, rival kings would have sought to take advantage of weaker rivals or expand their weakening agricultural base at their enemies' expense. Increasingly desperate armies likely came to resemble bandits, and their kings probably acted more like bandit captains. People may have turned to religion and then turned against it, desecrating temples and burning palaces, killing kings and priests. The population shrunk, not only from outright deaths from starvation, disease and war, but because in desperate and uncertain times when the world seemed to be falling apart, they likely had fewer children[52]. Those that did survive to carry on left the cities to avoid all the troubles, and in the process, Tikal and its rivals were ultimately reduced to ruins. When thinking about the Maya Collapse, many descriptions might come to mind, such as "tragic," "fascinating," and even "inevitable", but "enigmatic" and "mysterious" are not among them.

At the same time, it's clear that Tikal influenced later Mayan settlements. Besides its direct role in dominating the political and economic structure of the Mayan heartland during its periods of regional hegemony, Tikal had a much larger place in Mayan history as one of the fonts of the more sophisticated elements of Mayan culture. The first of these was serving as a political role model far beyond the areas it controlled. At its height, other Mayan cities' rulers took great pains to demonstrate their genealogical and ideological links to Tikal, even emulating the city's royal ceremony and regalia. This was especially true after the Teotihuacano Entrada, when the dynastic system was infused with the patriarchal systems and religious rituals and symbolism of Central Mexico. Even after the Collapse of Classical Mayan civilization, it seems that refugees who came to the northern Yucatan also brought this dynastic tradition (albeit with many changes) when they founded new cities like Uxmal, Chichén Itzá and Mayapán[53].

Furthermore, scribes in Tikal were at the forefront in transforming the incipient writing system they inherited from El Mirador and Nakbé into a sophisticated, fully-formed orthography capable of expressing all of the subtleties of human language. This remarkable feat - the creation of writing - has only been accomplished three times in human history: in Mesoamerica, Mesopotamia and China. The beautiful Mayan glyphs reached their fullest flower in Tikal and its neighboring cities, and even today, over 7,000 texts of varying length survive[54].

---

52 A modern example of this would be the massive population decline in the former Soviet Union states after the collapse of that government.
53 Pohl (1999), pg 73
54 Pohl (1999), pg07

Chapter 7: Modern Tikal

"The imagination reels. There are reliefs, pyramids, temples in the extinguished city. The damp murmur of the arroyos, voices, crepitations of the intertangling vines, the sound of flapping wings, trickle into the immense sea of silence. Everything palpitates, breathes, exhausting itself in green above the vast roof of Peten." - Miguel Ángel Asturias (1967 Nobel Laureate), in *The Mirror of Lida Sal: Tales Based on Mayan Myths & Guatemalan Legends*, p. 13-14.

The city of Tikal was abandoned, but it was never truly lost or forgotten. When the Spanish arrived in the Lake Peten Itzá area in the 1620s, they found the local Itzá Maya rulers from the nearby lake city of Tayasal worshiping at the ruins and venerating its builders, well aware that ancient Tikal's people were their ancestors[55]. In the Colonial period, it was occasionally visited by Spaniards and was certainly well-known by local hunters who regularly traveled through it on their treks.

The first Guatemalan government survey of the ruins was done in 1848, and this was followed by Eusebio Lara's drawings of stelae on the site, which attracted considerable attention. While Guatemala declared its independence in 1825, it was not until 1840 that it was fully independent of the United Provinces of Central America. Since the very beginning, Guatemala has sought to establish its national identity based in part upon a glorification of the ancient Mayan past, which is deeply troubling considering the great lengths that this same government has gone to keep down the Mayan peoples actually living in its territory, even to the point of an attempted genocide in the late 20th century. Despite these contradictions, the Guatemalan government has based much of its symbolism upon the Maya, including a Classical sculpture of a Mayan head on the 25 centavo coin and Tikal's Temple I on the back of the old 1/2 Quetzal note. [56]

In 1877, Europeans became increasingly interested in Tikal and the other ruins, especially after Austrian national Gustav Bernoulli visited the city and took a series of wood carved panels back home with him[57]. These panels, which were from Temples I and IV depicted, the life of Jasaw Chan K'awiil I, and while their plunder and movement to museums in Austria was certainly a theft from the Guatemalan people, it allowed the fragile wood to be preserved to the modern day. After Bernoulli, there were other expeditions. In 1881 and 1882 the English proto-archaeologist Alfred Maudslay made a map and survey of the city, and Teobert Maler took photos for the Peabody Museum[58]. From 1926-1937, Sylvanus Morley from Harvard University and the Carnegie Institute made surveys, and there has been an almost continuous period of work at Tikal since, including an elaborate 18 year project by the Guatemalan Government and the University of Pennsylvania[59].

---

55 Pohl (1999) pg 69
56 The Guatemalan currency is the "Quetzal".
57 An image of the panels can be seen here: http://www.allposters.com/-sp/A-Carved-Wood-Lintel-from-Temple-IV-at-Tikal-Collected-in-1877-by-the-Explorer-Gustav-Bernoulli-Posters_i10133629_.htm
58 Pohl (1999) pg 70
59 For a reconstruction of Tikal based upon Penn's work, visit:

In 1979, the site was given recognition by the United Nations Education, Science and Cultural Organization (UNESCO) as a "World Heritage Site"[60]. It did so on a number of overarching criteria that capture some of the ruins' importance to humanity; Tikal was selected "to represent a masterpiece of human creative genius; to bear a unique or at least exceptional testimony to a cultural tradition or to a civilization which is living or which has disappeared; to be an outstanding example of a type of building, architectural or technological ensemble or landscape which illustrates (a) significant stage(s) in human history…"

The site's ecological value, preserving a wide swath of forest as it does, is also recognized by UNESCO. In this regard, Tikal was selected "to be outstanding examples representing significant on-going ecological and biological processes in the evolution and development of terrestrial, fresh water, coastal and marine ecosystems and communities of plants and animals; to contain the most important and significant natural habitats for in-situ conservation of biological diversity, including those containing threatened species of outstanding universal value from the point of view of science or conservation."

Of course, Tikal is not simply a site of research or international recognition but also a premier tourist site today. Thousands of tourists come annually to marvel over the ruins of the once mighty city, helping ensure that the world's fascination with the Ancient Maya doesn't end anytime soon.

Bibliography

Berlin, Heinrich (April 1967). "The Destruction of Structure 5D-33-1st at Tikal". American Antiquity (Washington, D. C., USA: Society for American Archaeology) 32 (2): 241–242. ISSN 0002-7316. JSTOR 277915. OCLC 754651089. Retrieved 06-05-13. (subscription required)

Coe, Michael D. (1999). The Maya. Ancient peoples and places series (6th edition, fully revised and expanded ed.). London and New York: Thames & Hudson. ISBN 0-500-28066-5.

Drew, David (1999). The Lost Chronicles of the Mayan Kings. Los Angeles: University of California Press.

Gill, Richardson B. (2000). The Great Maya Droughts: Water, Life, and Death. Albuquerque: University of New Mexico Press. ISBN 0-8263-2194-1. OCLC 43567384.

Harrison, Peter D. (2006). "Maya Architecture at Tikal". In Nikolai Grube (ed.). Maya: Divine Kings of the Rain Forest. Eva Eggebrecht and Matthias Seidel (assistant eds.). Köln: Könemann. pp. 218–231. ISBN 3-8331-1957-8. OCLC 71165439.

Jones, Grant D. (1998). The Conquest of the Last Maya Kingdom. Stanford, California, USA:

http://www.penn.museum/sites/expedition/rebuilding-the-ruins/
60 "Tikal" at the World Heritage Site Homepage, accessed online at whc.unesco.org/en/list/64

Stanford University Press. ISBN 9780804735223. OCLC 38747674.

Kelly, Joyce (1996). An Archaeological Guide to Northern Central America: Belize, Guatemala, Honduras, and El Salvador. Norman: University of Oklahoma Press. ISBN 0-8061-2858-5. OCLC 34658843.

Looper, Matthew G. (1999). "New Perspectives on the Late Classic Political History of Quirigua, Guatemala". Ancient Mesoamerica (Cambridge and New York: Cambridge University Press) 10 (2): 263–280. doi:10.1017/S0956536199101135. ISSN 0956-5361. OCLC 86542758.

Looper, Matthew G. (2003). Lightning Warrior: Maya Art and Kingship at Quirigua. Linda Schele series in Maya and pre-Columbian studies. Austin: University of Texas Press. ISBN 0-292-70556-5. OCLC 52208614.

Martin, Simon; and Nikolai Grube (2000). Chronicle of the Maya Kings and Queens: Deciphering the Dynasties of the Ancient Maya. London and New York: Thames & Hudson. ISBN 0-500-05103-8. OCLC 47358325.

Martin, Simon; and Nikolai Grube (2008). Chronicle of the Maya Kings and Queens: Deciphering the Dynasties of the Ancient Maya (2nd (revised) ed.). London and New York: Thames & Hudson. ISBN 978-0-500-28726-2. OCLC 191753193.

Miller, Mary Ellen (1999). Maya Art and Architecture. London and New York: Thames & Hudson. ISBN 0-500-20327-X. OCLC 41659173.

Miller, Mary; and Karl Taube (1993). The Gods and Symbols of Ancient Mexico and the Maya: An Illustrated Dictionary of Mesoamerican Religion. London: Thames & Hudson. ISBN 0-500-05068-6. OCLC 27667317.

Schele, Linda; and Peter Mathews (1999). The Code of Kings: The language of seven Maya temples and tombs. New York: Simon & Schuster. ISBN 978-0-684-85209-6. OCLC 41423034.

Sharer, Robert J.; with Loa P. Traxler (2006). The Ancient Maya (6th, fully revised ed.). Stanford, CA: Stanford University Press. ISBN 0-8047-4817-9. OCLC 57577446.

Webster, David L. (2002). The Fall of the Ancient Maya: Solving the Mystery of the Maya Collapse. London: Thames & Hudson. ISBN 0-500-05113-5. OCLC 48753878.

Made in the USA
San Bernardino, CA
21 October 2015